TIME MANAGEMENT FOR MORTALS

Learn the successful habits needed to double your output in half the time, reach your goals without stress, and optimize your productivity.

Teddy Franco

Table of Contents

Introduction 1

Chapter 1: Time Is Of The Essence 3
    Understanding The Value Of Time 3
    Your Life Depends On How Well You Manage Your Time 5
    What Is Time Management And Why Does It Matter? 5
    The Principle Of Time Management 7
    Time Management Is A Workout 8
    You're Not Meant To Multitask 10
    Forget About Splitting Your Attention 12

Chapter 2: Managing Your Time Like A Leader 17
    Time Management And Leadership 17
    The Common Struggles With Time Management 20
    The Important Rules Of Time Management 25

Chapter 3: Productive Optimization 30
    But First, You Need To Tweak Your Brain 30
    Strategies To Be More Productive 34
    Setting Goals To Achieve 39

Chapter 4: One Thing At A Time 43
    Energy And Recovery 43
    How To Stay Focused And Manage Distractions 48
    Don't Procrastinate 51

Conclusion 56

Description 58

Introduction

Congratulations on purchasing *Time Management and Productivity* and thank you for doing so.

Nothing feels worse than reaching the end of a busy day, only to realize that you didn't get as much done as you hoped. It felt like you were busy running from one task to the next, and yet when you look at your to-do list, it seems as if you've barely made a dent. The chances are that you're probably struggling with your time management skills, and it is starting to affect your productivity levels too. When you're juggling between pressure and the stress of trying to get everything done, your productivity levels will slowly begin to dwindle. There's a very simple reason for that, and it is because productivity and stress cannot exist together. It is actually quite a vicious cycle when you think about it. When you're stress, you can't focus on what you're supposed to do. When you can't focus, your productivity levels take a nosedive. When that happens, you become even *more* stressed because the work is piling up, and you're struggling to muddle through it all.

It's a cycle that is going to keep spinning around and around until you do something to break it. The solution lies in learning how to better manage your time with the right time management strategies. Time is all we have. Time management is a concept that started out in philosophy. History shows that ancient philosophers have been obsessed with this one, very simple question: *How do we make the best use of the time we have in a way that makes our lives more meaningful?* That's a very good question indeed, and it is a concept that many people are struggling with until this day.

Why do we need to manage time? Some people say we need to learn how to manage time because we know that time is precious, and it should be used to its fullest potential if we hope to reap the benefits of time. Others might say that time is money, and that is why we need to manage it as best we can. Logically, if we did that, we should be maximizing our earning potential. The problem is, most people still find it hard to balance their time, even though they have tried in the past. The efforts never seem to stick, and that is the dilemma. If we *know* we need to better manage our time, *why aren't the habits we try to implement sticking*? Why do we keep falling back into old habits, and time continues to slip away from us?

Perhaps because the approach you've been taking wasn't the most effective one. To become the master of time management, you need to first *understand* the change you are trying to inflict in your life. Before you jump right in and start trying to implement all the strategies you can think of, you need to lay the foundation first. You lay that foundation by understanding *why* we struggle to manage time, what we've been doing wrong all this time, and *what* we can do moving forward so that this time, the change you're trying to create is going to stick around.

There are plenty of books on this subject on the market, thanks again for choosing this one! Every effort was made to ensure it is full of as much useful information as possible, please enjoy!

Chapter 1:

Time Is of the Essence

There is only one thing in your life that you can never get back once it is gone. It is not money, and it is not material items either. No, the one thing that you can never replace once the moment has passed is your *time*. You see, time is a very unique concept and an equally unique idea. When it is utilized correctly, it contains all the ingredients you need to lead a successful and productive life. When utilized correctly, you could have all the things in life that you ever dreamed of, like happiness, prosperity, growth, success, and so much more. At the same time, if it is neglected, time will pass you by, and it will leave you with very little.

Understanding the Value of Time

From the moment you wake up in the morning, you are living seconds, minutes, and hours that you will never be able to get back again. This is your one and only opportunity to embrace what you have at the moment. Every second, minute, and hour of your life is *precious* and it should be treated as such. When time ticks forward, precious moments are slipping away and they are taking with it the opportunity to make a difference. You need to hold on to each minute like your life depended on it, because you know what? It does! You never know when an hour could be the hour that you make a difference in yours or someone else's life, and this is why time is one of the most valuable assets you will ever own. This can mean only one thing. *There is NO perfect time to get anything done.* The time is *right now*, not tomorrow, not next week, and not sometime in the future. There is one mentality that we need to let go of if you want to march forward to a better, more productive way of life. The mentality that you need to disregard right now is the frame of mind that the *future* somehow means more than the present. There is no such thing as "saving the best" for another time.

Every moment that you have is precious, and every moment you have should be utilized to its fullest potential. Success comes from hard work and effort, better productivity, and time management. You need to allocate your time wisely if you hope to reap all the benefits that you desire. Every day is the day that you have the power to be powerful, successful, driven, and motivated. Every day is the day that you have the power to achieve a goal that you have always dreamed of. Every day is the day that you have the power to be more productive. There are no limits in life except the limits that you place on yourself. The only reason that you feel you're not accomplishing much is that your time is not being managed wisely. You are where you are in life right now because this is where you decided to be. Right now, you've decided to make a change for the better by figuring out a way to boost your productivity and improve your time management.

If you want to change, then the only person who can manufacture that kind of change is *you*. You've already taken the first step by using this book as your guide. We are in a very lucky position today. We live in a world where we have access to all the technology and information we could ever need. We have access to every tool and resource that we need to succeed.

The only thing stopping us is the ability to manage our time better. Time management is a power that you didn't know you had.

Your Life Depends On How Well You Manage Your Time

Motivational public speaker Brian Tracy once said this: *"A lack of clarity is the number one reason why we waste our time. We should always be asking ourselves what we are trying to do and HOW we are trying to do it."* The biggest problem that most people have today is "time poverty." Those who focus on work, work, work all the time have very little time for the other aspects of their life. They have too much to do when it comes to working that the other areas of their life begin to experience neglect and start to fall by the wayside. When this happens, people often wonder why achieving a well-rounded and balanced life seems like such an impossible concept. The truth is, it is *not* impossible at all. We're simply going about it the wrong way. If you're like most people, you're probably feeling overwhelmed by the activities and the many responsibilities you are trying to juggle. The more you struggle to catch up, the further behind you seem to fall. Instead of trying to decide what you want to do, you continue to react to the things that happen around you. In the process, you will get a lot more stressed out, and worked up than you should be. Eventually, you begin to lose all sense of control, and your brain shuts down completely. That is when your productivity and desire to do any kind of work comes to a complete standstill.

Time is your most precious resource, and it is your ability to manage your time wisely that is going to make the biggest difference in your life. It is perishable, it is irreplaceable, and once it is gone, there is no going back in time. You don't need a magic solution. What you need is a deeper understanding of the concept of time management.

What Is Time Management and Why Does It Matter?

All the work that you do in a day requires time. The very act of pausing for a moment to think about how you are going to use your time is already going to improve your time management and increase your productivity levels almost immediately. Time management describes the way a person purposefully plans for and organizes their time based on the specific tasks and activities that need to be accomplished. You could map out your time based on hours, days, weeks, or even months, depending on what works best for you. For example, when you are at work, you know you know have about eight hours to finish everything you need to do. It is your responsibility to divide your time the way you think you need to in order to finish all the tasks that must be done for the day. You get to decide how much time gets spent on each activity. In other words, you are in charge of your entire schedule for the day. Time management is not a business tool. It is not an app, a calculator, or a mobile phone that you can pick up and try to organize. Time management is *not* something that you use to increase your productivity in the hopes of being paid more money.

More importantly, time management is not a peripheral activity. Your time management abilities are the *core skills* upon which all your other skills will be built. In your work and personal life, there are going to be a lot of demands on your time and your skill. Most of these will be coming from the demands of other people, especially when you are at work. Very little of your time is actually yours to do with it what you wish. That happens when you're at work. When you are at home, however, that is a different story. You have a lot more control over your time when you're home, and you can easily use this time to increase your productivity in both your personal and professional life throughout the day. Time management allows you to focus on the tasks at hand to achieve the desired results. Just because a person looks "busy," it does not necessarily mean they are more productive or effective. Looking busy should not be the primary goal. When someone is rushing around the office in a frenzy or furiously clicking away at their keyboard with fervor, it doesn't necessarily mean they're handling their task as effectively as they should be. If you've ever found yourself in a situation where you felt like you were rushing about all day and yet felt at the end of the day that you hardly accomplished anything at all, this is the reason why. You were probably scrambling instead of trying to manage your time wisely.

The way you manage your time is something that only you have control over. Therefore, the change in your time management abilities and your productivity has to start from you. No one else can do this for you. When you've got good time management, the benefits you stand to gain will start showing themselves in all the other areas of your life without even knowing it. For one thing, you will find that you begin to experience less stress even though your workload may be as high as a mountain. You are far more productive and efficient, and the tasks you handle to achieve the desired results. Your reputation at work improves because you are viewed as efficient and effective. You are consistently on top of deadlines instead of rushing after them. Your workflow is more efficient and organized. Time management is not about how much time in a day you have, but rather it is about how well you organize the time you have been given. Everyone has the power within their hands to manage their time better with the proper techniques and strategies on how to do it. Time management is the key to developing the skills that you need to always stay one step ahead of your tasks instead of always falling behind.

The Principle of Time Management

There is a principle of time management that says, *"the hard time will push out the soft time."* This means that hard times, like when you are working hard, will push out the soft time that you have. Soft times could be times that you spend with your family or the time you choose to commit to yourself for a little bit of recovery and self-care. For example, if you don't finish everything that you need to do at the office because you are not managing your time well, you will invariably have to rob that borrowed time from other areas of your life, like quality time with your family. Since quality time with your family is precious to you, you're going to find yourself on a conflicting path. Effective time management encompasses several different aspects, among them include setting deadlines, setting your goals and objectives to be achieved per task, effectively planning for each task, being able to delegate responsibilities when needed, determining which tasks should be prioritized above all other tasks, and then *how much time* you should be spending per activity. *"What is the most valuable use of my time right now?"* is a question that you need to consistently ask when you find yourself with too much to do.

Time Management Is A Workout

Time management is hard work. If you think about it, we all have twenty-four hours in a day. That sounds like a lot when you say it out loud, and yet we still scramble to get things done. Deadlines start to pile up, and you've found yourself on more than one occasion wishing you had more than one pair of hands so you could handle everything all at once. Feeling pressed for time, feeling pressured because there never seems to be enough time to handle everything that needs to get done in a day, especially at work, is something that many people struggle with far too often. You don't need an extra pair of hands. What you need instead is better time management. Time management is a power that we all possess. The only trouble is that it is a power not everyone has been able to harness just yet because they don't know how. But once you begin to tap into this incredible ability to manage your own time, it will make a tremendous difference in your life. You'll work smarter instead of herder, you'll get this done without stretching yourself too thin, you feel less stress even with a heavy workload, and the biggest change of all will be how much more productive you become compared to the person you were before.

Since you can only do one thing at a time, consistent organization of your time is an ongoing process. This is why time management is hard work. You need to ensure that the *one thing* you are doing is *the most important thing* at any given time. When you learn how to manage your time better, you get to *choose* what you would like to work on first. In other words, when you wake up every morning, you should be ready to start planning out your day. Effectively planning your day starts with something as simple as preparing a to-do list of activities that need to be done for the day. To be as effective as you possibly can, you must place all the important and top priority tasks should always be, well, at the top of the list. A to-do list is an essential part of the time management process because it makes your job a whole lot easier when you don't have to keep scrambling and trying to recall what you might have missed for the day. Arranging them in order of priority simplifies the process even further. Once you're done with a task, simply cross it off your list and finish the rest of the tasks on that list with peace of mind knowing that *the* most important tasks for the day have already been done and dusted. It keeps you from feeling overwhelmed too.

Time management may be hard work, but it is going to allow you to organize every aspect of your life. That way, you get the greatest joy, happiness, and satisfaction out of everything that you do. The best thing you can do for yourself to transform your levels of productivity is to simply learn the crucial art of time management and making it work to your advantage. You have it in you to produce work that is consistent and work that is nothing but top-notch quality. You have the power to churn out your very best work *all the time* if you only learn how to manage your time wisely.

You no longer have to be stifled by the bad habit of waking up each day with a "rough idea" of what you should and need to accomplish today. You don't need to "go with the flow" or "wing it" and hope that you scrape by on the bare minimum. All it takes is a simple tweak that involves effectively planning out your day down to the little details. That one tiny change is going to create a ripple effect that will bring about big changes in your productivity levels. At the end of the day, it is possible to feel accomplished and satisfied, and it is absolutely possible to feel like this *every single day.*

You're Not Meant to Multitask

Life is short, and we should be maximizing every moment that we have. Achieving maximum efficiency is not about working non-stop until you're too tired to even stand up straight anymore. Being efficient with your time means that you're going to have the time you want to do *everything* you want in a day, week, or month without feeling burned out in the process. The is the first principle toward becoming efficient, productive, and effective. The problem is that we think we can do it all, but the truth is that we should only be focusing on one task at a time. *That is how you maximize every moment.* Have you ever been guilty of trying to do work while you were watching a movie? How did that work out for you? That's not an effective use of your time. We either need to focus on work or focus on play, but never focus on trying to do both at the time there. There is no middle ground that you can place yourself in, and for one simple reason. The human mind was not made for multitasking. Go back to the example of trying to get your work done while you're in front of the TV or your iPad watching a movie. The quality of your work is compromised, and you're not fully enjoying the movie either because you're not entirely focused on it. In the end, both activities become compromised, and you achieve nothing in either activity. You didn't enjoy the movie like you hoped you would, and the document you were working on is not as good as you know it should be. Trying to multitask is simply not a good use of your time.

You could spend years trying to find that ever-elusive work-life balance. The reason you are going to spend years trying to chase this concept but never achieving it is that *the concept does not exist*. Work-life balance is nothing more than a myth. The reality is that these two concepts are something that we continually bounce back and forth from in the greater context of our lives. There will be some days when you're working hard and some days when you are playing hard. Effective time management is about prioritizing between your tasks. The foundation begins by first sitting down and taking a long, hard look at how you are currently spending your time. Evaluate it with honesty because only then will you be able to see where improvement needs to be made. For example, squeezing a workout into your busy schedule at the end of each day might not seem urgent, but it is important, and it should be placed as a priority in your schedule since it has compounding effects on your long-term health.

Better time management will eventually lead to better productivity when you learn how to evaluate your time better. Evaluate how you spend the time that you have right now. When planning for your tasks during the day, consider the goals that you have in mind for each task. The goals you set will help you decide how much effort and focus you need to put into each task. It will also help you ascertain what priority each task on your list should have. For example, if a task is going to require a lot of time, but the main goal or outcome of the task is not on top priority, then that task should be on the bottom of your list. The main idea behind the concept of time management and productivity is figuring out the little areas of your life that you could be maximizing on. You're trying to figure out how you can include the tasks you need to finish during the day and where they best fit into the allotted time that you have. One example that could illustrate this point is the commute that you make daily to work. Are you maximizing the time that you spend here? Instead of feeling bored on your ride to work, you could be listening to a podcast you have been putting off, or perhaps read a chapter of a book you have been meaning to get to. You see how that works? You're killing off two birds with one stone in this example *and* the best part is that you are not wasting any time at all. For example, if it was on your to-do list to read a chapter of a book for the day, then you could easily cross it off your list by the time you arrive at work. A simple but efficacious way to maximize your time, wouldn't you say?

Forget About Splitting Your Attention

We were simply not designed for multitasking despite what the many apps, websites, and blogs out want you to believe. Your best work happens when you stay completely focused on what you are supposed to be doing, and this includes moments of play. Splitting your focus is only going to wreak havoc on *both* your work and play. When you're supposed to be working on your deadline for work, but you end up picking up your phone to scroll through your latest notifications, you're procrastinating and compromising your productivity. When you're grabbing dinner with a friend but can't resist the urge to check the notifications on your phone again, you're not enjoying your friend's company and miss important bits of the story they were telling you. Did you happen to notice that when it was the day before the deadline of your college assignment back when you were studying, you got more done in a day than you did in the last three weeks that you had to work on that assignment? Interestingly enough, that is Parkinson's Law at work. This particular law states that *work expands to fill the time that has been allotted to it.* When we are faced with a looming deadline, suddenly we find that we become more productive because we are forced to maintain our focus on the task.

Imagine what it would be like if you never have to wait until the final day before something is due and *yet* still enjoy the benefits of being focused and productive. This is absolutely possible, but first, you are going to have to forget about multitasking altogether. Forget about the gurus and life hackers who claim that multitasking is the answer to better productivity. *It is not.* Multitasking is ineffective in the long-run and rather than promote better concentration it promotes anxiety instead. Chasing the clock was never an effective strategy toward becoming more productive. All that is going to do is make you more anxious, nervous, stressed, and flustered. Those feelings will only magnify when you keep checking the clock and see the deadline ticking closer, only to realize that you have barely made a dent in your work. Your focus is going to dissipate under this self-imposed and unrealistic deadline. When you're stressed and flustered, this is when you run the risk of making one too many mistakes. You begin to overlook crucial information, you slip up and get the documents mixed up, maybe you even send an email to the wrong person. You're becoming increasingly more agitated as you try to rush to meet your deadline goal in the hopes of quickly moving on to the next task. Multitasking is and always has been one of the biggest mistakes we have allowed ourselves to believe for far too long. It's counterproductive and it clutters your mind.

Multitasking is a term that was first used in the 60s to describe a computer's performance. However, the human brain is *not* like a computer. We can't have multiple tabs open in the brain at once and still hope to execute each tab perfectly. Unlike the computer, the human brain's attention is a very limited resource. If you stretch it too thin, you're going to lose the ability to focus altogether. Multitasking means your attention and focus is pulled in several directions all at once. To be focused and productive, however, you are required to only focus on one thing at a time. The demanding and hectic pace of today's lifestyle has led to the false belief that you're increasing your productivity when you multitask. Nothing could be further from the truth. Our minds were only made to focus on one thing, one stimulus at a time. If you could visualize your attention span as if it were a spotlight, then you know that the spotlight can only be shone on one place at any given time. Well, that is how some psychologists describe the human brain's attention span anyway. Multitasking is not for everyone. If someone you know may be doing it, it doesn't necessarily mean it may be as effective for you as it is for them. When you try to handle more than a single task at a time, you either can't or won't do either task well. You think you're trying to save time, but really all you're doing is hampering your productivity.

If you wanted proof that the human mind can only focus on one thing at a time, then look no further than the *Gorilla Experiment.* When participants of the experiment were asked to concentrate on how many times the basketball players who were dressed in white passed the ball, the participants of the experiment completely missed out on the fact that at some point during the game, a gorilla walked past. This is proof that the human brain simply does not have the capacity to process everything at once. The pressure of juggling multiple responsibilities has turned multitasking into an acceptable thing these days, and that is an ongoing mistake that is costing us our productivity. There are numerous articles on the Internet that will try to convince you multitasking is a prized skill. Some employers even list it as part of the job requirements when interviewing new candidates. This false perception that multitasking is acceptable has only increased the amount of pressure and stress that is felt. When you're always feeling the pressure and the stress, it is going to be nearly impossible to be productive at the same time. Our brains have a deliberate system, and while we may think we're handling tasks and completing them in a parallel manner, what the brain is actually doing is switching your attention back and forth between each activity. When you move from one task to the next, you can't pick up where you left off. We can switch our attention from one task to the next and back again, but when our attention span becomes overloaded, that is when you start to miss things that could be right under our nose. A professor from the University of Minnesota, Sophie Leroy, introduced the concept of attention residue back in 2009. Leroy's research discovered that when you move from A to B, your attention does not immediately do the same thing. While you're already getting started on B, your mind is still lingering on A, meaning that your attention is divided, and you're not as focused as you think you are. The only time it is possible to do two things at once is if both these activities require a different set of cognitive resources.

One example of when it might be okay to multitask is when you're reading a book while listening to music. This is because those two activities engage a different set of resources in the brain. Driving and talking on the phone, however, is an example of when multitasking doesn't work. True, it may seem as if both these activities require a different set of cognitive resources, but research has revealed that we have a tendency to create mental images when we are talking on the phone. This means that we could be looking right at a hazard but fail to see it, causing accidents along the way that could have easily been prevented. If multitasking is just going to make you feel more overwhelmed than ever, then what you're doing is going to be counterproductive instead of productive. Don't try to handle several things at once if this style of working isn't a good fit for you then focus on one thing at a time and get it done before moving onto the next if it's going to make you more productive. Multitasking makes us inefficient at best, and at worst, it makes us downright dangerous. Just like the example of what happens when you drive and talk on the phone, even if it is hands-free while you do it. If you want to better manage your time and boost your productivity, forget about the urge to try and do ten things at once. That is just *not* how your brain was wired.

Chapter 2:

Managing Your Time Like a Leader

The way you manage your time can change the way that you work as an individual and as a leader. Time management and leadership are about shifting your perspective about *what time management involves* rather than thinking about all the tasks you need to do. Look at some of the richest people in the world. Sometimes, you can't help but wonder how they managed to accomplish a lot with the same twenty-four hours we have been given. How did they come up with the winning strategy that allowed them to effectively maximize their time in such a way that they become extremely successful leaders?

Time Management and Leadership

It is no secret that successful leaders take advantage of the snippets of time they have been given. Effective time management encompasses several different aspects. Among them include setting deadlines, setting your goals and objectives to be achieved per task, effectively planning for each task, being able to delegate responsibilities when needed, determining what tasks should be prioritized above all other tasks. They also think about how much time they should be spending per activity. In between all of that, they find a way to maximize their time by using the little snippets of free time that they have productively. Everyone has little snippets of free time in between the tasks that they do, and how well you're effectively utilizing that time makes all the difference in the world.

Leaders value their time and they take it very seriously. You will never find a successful leader wasting precious time and energy doing something that is not meaningful. A leader never wakes up every morning with a "rough idea" of what they need to finish today. They don't wake up in the morning and decide that they are going to go with the flow and hope to accomplish most of their tasks along the way. That is because a leader values every single minute that they have. They know that every minute is another minute that they could spend making a difference. That minute could be spent bringing them one step closer to their goals or making a difference in their life or someone else's. There is only one thing on this earth that money cannot buy, and that is *your time*.

Every successful leader lives by this golden rule, and that is why they focus their time on the most productive and meaningful tasks on their to-do list during the day. A small tweak like effectively planning for your day is a small tweak that can bring about big changes in your productivity and the way that you feel at the end of the day, as well as how much you manage to accomplish at the end of it. Be on the lookout each day for ways you can maximize your time, leveraging every advantage that is at your disposal. Adopt a positive approach to this too because the more positively you approach the tasks you have been given, the better the outcome will be. A positive approach will always outperform a negative one because negativity will only serve to distract you, make you lose focus, and at the end of the day you feel as if time has just slipped through your fingers and nothing on your task list has been effectively accomplished the way you wanted it to be. Most people are focused on how they can make more money instead of focusing on how they should be utilizing their time. When you have time, you can *always* make money as long as you continue to provide value to someone who is willing to pay for it.

A successful leader is always thinking about long-term goals and the bigger picture. That is how they managed to invest their time wisely, making all the right decisions to get them to the position they find themselves in today. Bill Gates once said this: *"We often overestimate the change that will happen in the next two years and underestimate the change that will happen in the next ten years."* The trouble with most people and a lot of leaders is the failure to think about the long-term benefits. A lot of leaders, especially the newer ones, make the mistake of forgetting to focus on the bigger picture. The concept of time management is essentially about balance, a balance you must find within the process of planning how to juggle the myriad of activities and tasks that you are faced with each day. Unfortunately, most people succumb to the allure of instant gratification. We all want results, and we want to see results quickly. When something takes too long and requires a long-term effort, many people give up and quit along the way because they don't see the visible results that they were hoping for.

An effective leader is someone who balances your time and structures your day. Every single minute of your day from the moment you wake up needs to count for something. Time is precious, and not a single moment should be wasted. Finding that balance between work, family, a social life, health and fitness, personal commitments, your own interests, and any other demands that may command your attention means you need to find a way to prioritize all the different aspects. That way, you don't finish the end of the day feeling completely drained of energy yet at the same time feeling like you didn't accomplish everything that you wanted to. How well you manage your time each day will determine your successes and failures in life. The ones who achieve the most are the ones who have perfected the art of time management, maximizing each day to their fullest potential without compromising on the tasks at hand. Time is such a valuable asset because once a moment, or even a minute is gone, you can never get it back again. If you make every single minute of your day count, you will be amazed at how much you can accomplish.

The Common Struggles with Time Management

One of the biggest reasons why tasks seem to slip through the cracks is because we forget to write them down or set a reminder. Perhaps you're feeling extremely overwhelmed because you have said "yes" to far too many commitments, and now you feel like you are being stretched too thin. Many people can relate to these common scenarios because they are some of the most common time management mistakes. As a leader, it is very easy to find yourself overcommitted to too many tasks and responsibilities. Feeling overwhelmed is only going to cause stress, lower your productivity, and impact both the quality of your work and your leadership capabilities. That is why it is important to identify these time management mistakes. That way, you will be able to overcome them moving forward. Without identifying the problem, it is difficult to determine how you could change your time management skills for the better. Do any of these common time management struggles sound familiar to you?

- **You're Not Clear About the Project Details** - When the details of the projects and tasks you need to work on are not clear, what follows next is a lot of confusion and time-wasting. This is why a lack of clarity about what you're supposed to do is one of the common time management challenges that many faces and not just leaders alone. When you're not clear about the who, what, where, when, and why of any task that you undertake, a lot of time is going to be wasted trying to scramble for the details. This is precious time that could have been spent working on your project and getting ahead of schedule. Without project clarity, another problem presents itself. That problem is unrealistic expectations. When the details are hazy, the people involved in the project are going to assume their own deadlines. They're going to have certain expectations, and they expect you to meet those expectations. When deadlines are set up without calculating the required time and resources, the pressure to perform becomes a lot more stressful than it should be. Before you commit, you need to analyze each task that you have in front of you and then set a realistic time frame for how long you would need to complete it. Don't set a timeline that you think should be the right one or that you think you can squeeze through, look at the task objectively and realistically decide how much time should be allocated to this task depending on how much work is going to be involved or how complicated the task is. Otherwise, it is not a good use of your time and productivity.

- **You're Not Utilizing Your To-Do List Effectively** - A to-do list is there for a reason. When you don't write things down, it is easy to forget what you need to do. A to-do list is more than just a list and it is your tool for staying organized and staying on top of everything that you need to do. When tasks begin to slip through the cracks, people get disappointed, and your workload begins to pile up. Deadlines get missed, and everything starts to go south because the stress makes it feel like everything is snowballing out of control. It may be tedious, and it may feel like an extra effort, but a to-do list is critical to helping you manage your time better. It may seem easy to think that you'll be able to remember in your mind everything that you're supposed to be doing and what you need to do, but if that strategy hasn't worked in the past, it's not going to work now either. This is where your to-do list is going to come in handy once again (isn't it remarkable how simple yet effective these things are?). There is no better way to effectively prioritize everything that you need to do than a to-do list. It ensures that nothing will ever slip through the cracks and you will never have to feel stressed about missing out on another deadline again. Every leader knows the power of a good to-do list and since you are in a leadership position, this is something you should always have with you. You will undoubtedly have double the workload because people expect more from a leader. You naturally have more responsibility to juggle, and with people counting on you, you must always at the top of your game.

- **You're Not Prioritizing Your Tasks** - Certain tasks should take priority over the others. This will eliminate the other mistake of spending too much time on tasks that are not as important. Each task should be accompanied by a goal that you want to achieve by the end of this task. Setting goals is more important than you think, and it is because setting goals often go underestimated. Setting goals for every task you take on gives you a direction to head towards. Just like driving. When you know where you're going, it makes it easier to get there quicker and more effectively. As a leader, your time management skills must be one of your best skills. Otherwise, you could end up looking "busy" without anything actually getting done. When you get your priorities in order, it will minimize all the stress you feel when you see a long list of things that need to get done.

- **You're Tackling All the Most Difficult Tasks First Thing In The Morning** - Although it is good to try and get the difficult stuff out of the way first, it can be counterproductive to your productivity levels. Imagine that you're going for a run. In the beginning, you're pumped and full of energy, bursting through the first stage of your run with power in every stride. What happens to your body once it starts to get tired after a while? Your muscles start to get tired, you slow down, and your energy gradually begins to wane. Each step doesn't have as much power as it did when you first started your run. The same thing happens when you try to tackle all the hard tasks of the day first instead of pacing yourself. If you try to do too much too soon, your body's energy levels are going to start to drop. Once it begins to do that, your mind is going to have a hard time staying focused, and your productivity levels are going to suffer.

- **You're Not Managing Distractions** - This mistake could end up costing you hours of wasted time every day. The multiple phone calls and texts during the day, the endless notifications that keep popping up on your phone, quick chats with colleagues, several coffee breaks in a day, all those add up, and you suddenly realize that you've lost more time than you should in a day getting nothing done. If you want to be in control and the master of your own time, it starts with eliminating all the distractions you currently have around you. Take a break after you've completed a task, but avoid being distracted before. As a leader, you must be able to manage your interruptions and turn off your notifications when you need to focus and concentrate. Remove anything that might even be potentially distracting from your workspace, keep your phone silent during the time blocks you have allocated for yourself when you're working on it, and commit to not letting any distractions take your attention away from what you're supposed to be doing. Distractions are always going to be there unless you actively do something about it.

- **You Don't Know How to Say "No"** - It never feels good to have to say no to a request because you don't want to end up hurting the person's feelings. However, saying "yes" when you should be saying "no" is not going to bode well for your time management and productivity levels either. It is impossible to feel productive when you're feeling overwhelmed and stressed. Not to mention the fact that when you overextend yourself, you don't have the time or energy to do your best work.

- **You're Trying to Multitask** - This is one bad habit that absolutely needs to be broken because it is costing you valuable time and energy. We have established in the previous chapter that the human brain simply was not meant to multitask. It is going to take you much longer to do your work when you try to accomplish more than one task at a time. When you can't concentrate properly on one task, you're not performing at your best, and both tasks are going to come out poorly. This is obviously not going to reflect well on you as a leader, and this is one time management mistake that is best avoided at all cost.

- **You're Not Setting A Maximum Limit for Your Tasks** - The purpose of time management is not to try and take on all the tasks at once. The purpose of time management is to focus on channeling your resources to the tasks that are going to bring about the biggest benefit or biggest impact. If the tasks you choose to take on don't seem to be making much progress, then perhaps it wasn't the right task to focus on yet. Trying to do too much in a short period of time is going to have very negative implications on both your physical and psychological health.

The Important Rules of Time Management

As a leader, you're always going to feel like you're *too busy,* and when you're busy, every task your juggling feels like a game of pinball. At the end of the day, it is easy to feel like you were bouncing around from one task to another. Yet, you still have this nagging feeling in the back of your mind that you could have done a lot more. You go home thinking about work, and sometimes you end up bringing your work home with you because you're not satisfied with how much you managed to do during the day. That's pretty much like playing pinball, where you're haphazardly hitting and pressing all the buttons, hoping that you don't drop the ball along the way. If you spend time at the arcade, though, you will notice the more experienced pinball players who seem to effortlessly keep the game going. They had a *strategy* to make it work in their favor, and that is what you need to create with your time. A proper strategy a few time management rules will help you make the most of your time and become the effective leader you want to be. Just like the game of pinball, you're going to be randomly hitting stuff, hoping that you're going to get lucky along the way if you don't have a proper structure for your time. This brings us to the important rules of time management.

Before we get into the rules, you will notice that time management has several recurring themes. The themes are about setting goals for your tasks, and then creating a plan for your tasks based on the order of priority, and finally creating an environment that is conducive to your productivity. For a leader, here are the most important time management rules that are going to bring about the biggest change:

- **The One and Two Rule** - A successful leader begins their day by starting on the first and second tasks that take the highest priority of the day. The one and two rules are about choosing two tasks out of your entire to-do list for the day, and then start your day by focusing on only those two tasks first. This is an important time management concept, especially when you are aiming to accomplish multiple goals and outcomes within a day. It is necessary to then determine what goals are the most important out of all the goals you have set for yourself for that day, and this will give you the focus that you need to achieve these goals. Once that is done, you can move on to other items on your to-do list, *but not before* you get your number one and number two tasks done first. Goals and priorities are going to be the two keywords to focus on with this rule. Priorities will help you determine what tasks should be tackled first for the day that would yield the most beneficial results overall. With your goals and priorities in place, you won't make the mistake of spending too much time on tasks with minimal goal outcomes, and that everything that is important and requires urgent attention doesn't go unnoticed or gets forgotten. Focus on the two tasks of the day first and devise a strategy as to how you are going to accomplish them.

- **You Need to Start Delegating** - Some new leaders might be worried about coming off as too bossy by asking other people to handle some of the tasks on hand, but there is a difference between delegating and being bossy. The first thing you need to do is think about the tasks that are taking up too much of your time and resources. In any job that you have, over time, you are bound to inherit certain duties and responsibilities that happened along the way from the time you were hired. Once you got promoted, you inherited even *more* responsibilities while still keeping the tasks you had in your original role. As a leader, your focus and your priorities are going to change, and it's time to think about how best you can allocate your resources. You have a team of people for a reason, and you are not meant to handle everything all on your own. Periodically, you need to take a moment to evaluate how your day is progressing. If you're starting to notice certain tasks need to be picked up on, delegate the job to a team member or two that can help you take on the task and get it done by the deadline. Learning to delegate is something you need to start getting comfortable with. When a task needs an extra pair of hands, then delegating is something that needs to be done. You are not bossy because you're working on your own important deadlines for the team too. A good leader is working hard while ensuring that the rest of the team works well together to accomplish goals as a unit. Learning to delegate necessary tasks will prove to be a more productive move moving forward. Delegate to the right people and you will achieve results in a much shorter amount of time, and this will then leave you with more time to handle other tasks in turn. Learn to delegate responsibilities when needed by determining what tasks should be prioritized above all other tasks, and how much time you should be spending per activity.

- **Plan Your Day to Eighty Percent Capacity** - Another rule that every effective leader needs to follow is the rule *not* to keep themselves *too busy*. When you're too busy and packed with things to do the entire day, you'll be missing a lot of important deadlines. Just because you're the leader, it doesn't mean you need to have a full plate to be worthy of your title. A good leader understands that missing deadlines is never a good sign, and they make it a habit not to take on *too many* projects or commitments at once. Instead of planning a daily schedule that is packed to capacity, they make it a rule to plan a schedule to eighty percent capacity instead of the full one hundred percent. Does this make them less effective as a leader?

Not at all. In fact, by keeping that twenty percent free, it gives them leeway to handle any buffer items that might come up. Nothing is going to throw you off schedule quicker than an unexpected and urgent task, and if you don't schedule enough time in your day to manage these unexpected tasks, you're not going to meet the goals and deadlines that you originally set at the start of your day.

- **Come Fully Prepared** - When you sit down to start work on your task, you should be fully prepared with everything that you need. The most effective way to quickly knock off each task on your to-do list is to ensure you have everything that you will need on hand. This way, you don't have to stop your tasks halfway through and risk losing your focus because you forgot something that you need. When you are fully prepared, nothing is going to interrupt you until the task is done. A powerful motivator to stay on tasks and boost productivity levels is to be fully prepared all the time, no matter how big or small the task is.

- **Understand The Distinction Between "Urgent" and "Important"** - This rule is going to help you out when the time comes for you to assign a priority to each task. Not every task is going to be urgent, and not every urgent task is important. This is one of the rules that a lot of new leaders struggle with at the beginning. Understanding the distinction between these two terms is your first step towards harnessing the power of effective time management, and this applies not just at work but in everyday life too. Important tasks are obviously the tasks that matter, and not completing these important tasks could bode serious repercussions for you and possibly other people around you. This is especially prominent in a work environment setting, where every inaction could have a serious impact and potentially detrimental consequences on your performance and perception as an employee. Urgent tasks, on the other hand, would be the tasks that demand your immediate attention, but the difference here is that whether you actually complete the task or not may or may not matter because the consequences of leaving the task unfinished may not be as severe. The distinctions between "urgent" and "important" will form the basis of every goal and priority that you set for your tasks.

- **Follow the "Salami Slicing" Rule** - Unless you were really hungry, you wouldn't try to eat an entire loaf of salami all at once because you know it would be too much to handle. A loaf of salami is best enjoyed when it is sliced into little bite-size pieces that are easily digestible. Likewise, you don't have to try and handle a job all at once. Sometimes, the very best way for you to complete a major task is to "slice it like a salami" into smaller portions. Breaking the task down into smaller pieces and working on just that piece alone could be more productive than trying to handle a big, overwhelming task all at once. This is a difficult one for a lot of leaders to manage since as a leader, you know what you want and what you want to accomplish. However, setting goals that are far too big will only serve to overwhelm you, and it will then become counterproductive towards helping you manage your time efficiently. Instead, set smaller, achievable action goals that gradually lead up to the bigger goal instead. The same way you would take only a single slice of salami and eat that first before you see if you can manage anything else. When you choose to focus on only a small piece of the task first and discipline yourself to only focus on that task, it gives you the momentum you need to counter procrastination and inertia. Leaders are just as susceptible to procrastination as everyone else every now and then.

Chapter 3:

Productive Optimization

Here's a question to ponder for a minute: *What do you think about when you see the word "productivity?"* Perhaps you visualize a full list of tasks that have already been crossed off. Perhaps when you think about productivity, you think about getting into a steady state of focus and work flows smoothly. Time seems to pass you by because you're "in the zone" as you work through one task after the next without breaking momentum. No matter what productivity means to you, it is something that you can achieve. You see, productivity is not a course of action. *It is a state of mind.*

But First, You Need to Tweak Your Brain

If something is a state of mind, then it can absolutely be changed if you pushed your brain and trained it in the right manner. Lazy people can one day become some of the most hardworking people you will ever meet because they trained their brains to mimic the right habits. In short, they rewire their brains to become more productive. You were not lacking in productivity because you were lazy or incompetent. No, you were not productive because you didn't start with tweaking your brain and training it to become the productive version of yourself that you desire.

Before you get to work on the strategies to become more productive, you need to first train your brain to become receptive to these habits. How do you do that? This brain-tweaking framework will get you started:

- **Train Your Brain to Be an Early Riser** - Sunlight tells our brains when it is time to get up and rise in the morning and when it is time to wind down and call it a day. If you want to become more productive, you need to start training your brain to mimic this rhythm. Set your alarm to wake up when the sun rises in the morning or earlier if you think you need a little bit more time to get things done. You see, when we sleep at night, our body goes through different cycles. Waking up during the right cycles could mean the difference between feeling groggy and irritable and feeling refreshed, ready to seize the day.

- **Train Your Brain to Delay Gratification** - The ability to delay instant gratification is the key that separates successful people from the ones who tried to succeed and failed. Most people find it hard to resist temptation, and they end up succumbing to instant gratification in the short-term. Believe it or not, your inability to resist instant gratification is a contributing factor as to why you procrastinate so much. Procrastination is an irrational decision to delay doing something. We call it an irrational decision because even though we know we know what we should be doing, we choose to purposely postpone or delay it. We may even choose to do something else, thereby procrastinating. If we look at most forms of procrastination closely, we will realize that it is a choice for instant gratification over future reward or suffering. You need to train your brain to become comfortable with the idea of overlooking short-term pleasure because the long-term rewards are going to be worth the wait. This is a choice that needs to be made every single day, and it is not going to be easy, that is the truth. You will struggle to try to get your brain to cooperate, but eventually, it will become a habit once you observe how your productivity and focus are going to change for the better.

- **Do Something You Don't Want to Do** - Another exercise in training your brain to become more receptive to productivity is to do something you don't want to do. The moment you feel like you don't want to do something is the *precise moment* you should force yourself to do it. By forcing your brain to become comfortable with the idea of discomfort, you're indirectly training it to avoid procrastination in the future. If you have a task that you've been sitting on for a while and you're still reluctant to get started, *get up and force yourself to do it anyway*. Forget about how you feel and focus instead of getting the task done and out of the way. You don't have to feel happy about it, and you don't have to enjoy the entire process at all. The whole point is that you *do it anyway*, regardless of how you feel. That is how you break your brain out of the bad habit that it has been clinging to for far too long. By forcing yourself to persevere with this exercise, you are sending a signal to your body and your brain a very strong message. It is a message that you are going to steadfastly focus on what you want, and nothing is going to stop you from reaching that goal.

- **Do *Even More* Work During Your Peak Energy Moments** - Before you map out your day based on your to-do list, think about when you are at your most productive. Are you a night owl or early bird? Different people are productive at different times. Productivity does not mean that you *must* get everything done in the morning and during the day, no "ifs" and "buts" about it. That's not the way it works, and it is common misconceptions like those that keep you trapped in the same cycle of bad habits that hold you back. Not everyone is going to have the same preference for the time of day when they feel the most productive. Some might feel a lot more productive first thing in the morning while others do their best work at night. The point is, to make the most out of your productive streak, the key is to tap into the time of day when you feel the most energetic. When you're feeling energized, you're naturally more productive and this is where you should attempt to accomplish most of the tasks on your list before that streak dwindles. During your peak energy levels are also right about the same time you should attempt to tackle all the important tasks on your list. Your mind is sharp, your focus is spot-on, and this is where you are going to produce your best work.

- **Train Your Brain for Mindful Awareness** - We function on autopilot so often during the day that it has become second nature. Making a conscious effort to stop, pause, and tune in to your surroundings is something new. It is something that your brain is not used to before, and this is going to be a refreshing change of pace. At random moments during the day, stop and force your brain to tune in to your surroundings. What do you see? What do you hear? What are you doing right now? What sensations do you feel throughout your body? How do the clothes you're wearing feel against your skin? If you were working on a task, have you been reading the words in front of you? Or were you distracted by other thoughts? Mindfulness is an exercise that will train your brain to stay in control and on top of your thoughts all day long. When you're not functioning on autopilot all the time, you're less likely to succumb to distractions and procrastination because you're paying attention to what you do. Most of the time, when we procrastinate, we don't realize how much time has slipped away from us. Suddenly, a couple of hours have gone by, and you panic because you didn't realize what time it was. Mindfulness is one way to start training your brain to pay attention to what you do all day long. When you're paying attention, procrastination levels dip, and productivity levels soar.

Strategies to Be More Productive

If you think about it, productivity is a lot like exercise. You're running in the right direction for as long as you possibly can until you achieve your desired goal. Productivity is about making the biggest progress toward your goals in the shortest amount of time. You only have a limited amount of energy that you can expand each day. As you go about your daily activities, your energy bar is going to drop lower and lower, similar to the way your phone battery drops the longer you use it. The reason that a lot of your days have been ending with nothing to show for it is that you haven't been paying attention to the way you expand this energy. Everyone has the same twenty-four hours in a day, and you get to decide how you want to invest this time. You can choose to invest in your goals or you can go about your day hoping for the best outcome. If you want to make the most out of your day, you need the right strategies in place to boost your productivity levels. After you've done what you can to tweak your brain, it is now time to *work with your brain* and focus on the strategies that are going to make you a more productive person.

- **Write It Down** - Even if it isn't a to-do list per se, if something pops into your mind, make it a habit of writing it down before you forget it. You know that to-do lists are mandatory for increasing productivity, but you should also get into the habit of writing down something that pops into your mind suddenly, especially if it's a task that needs to be done. You could always pop it onto your to-do list later, or add it to a new to-do list if you want, depending on the urgency and importance of the task in question. When you write it down, especially if it is on a to-do list, it gives your brain something to focus on. The visual aid tells your brain that this is the direction you need to do, and this is what you need to do to get there. We are visual creatures by nature, and we tend to focus on what is in front of us since our perception is primarily rooted based on sight. What we consistently see in front of us is what helps to shape, condition, and develop our mindset. If you constantly see a list that gives you a sense of direction about the tasks that need to be done, it is going to train your brain to get focused from the moment you wake up in the morning. Plus, a list of things to do ensures that you don't waste precious minutes every morning thinking about what you need to do.

- **Don't Keep Adding Unnecessary Items to Your To-Do List -** When preparing your to-do list, you're going to be tempted to keep adding items that were *not* on the original list you prepared. If the tasks were not on your original to-do list for the day, consider whether the task is important enough to be added on at the last minute. If you keep adding unnecessary items to the list, it is either going to make you feel very frustrated at the end of the day when your list still seems like a mile-long despite the hard work you put in during the day. If you have to add things to your original to-do list, keep it to a maximum of no more than two or three items and save the rest for tomorrow. This is where priorities come into play.

- **Cut-Out Distractions Completely -** If you can't completely isolate yourself to focus on your tasks, then the next best thing you can do is to make it a habit from now on to cut-out distractions. The brain is only capable of focusing on one task at a time, and you need to minimize the distractions that might happen while you're busy working on your task. There are some distractions that are within your power to control, like turning off your mobile devices and all other notifications until you're finished with what you do. Emails and phone calls don't need to be answered straight away unless that is your job. Otherwise, they can wait until you're finished with the task. Don't forget that the brain is not built to switch quickly from one task to the next because this is actually going to lower your productivity instead of helping it. You don't need to check your social media notifications every twenty minutes. You'll be a lot more productive if you don't have all these distractions going on.

- **Keep Your Workspace Organized** - *"A place for everything and everything in its place"* should be your new productivity mantra when you're organizing your workspace. When everything is arranged neatly on your desk, it becomes a lot easier to focus on the task at hand, especially when you're not distracted by the urge to sort through the messy pile of papers on your desk. When you don't have to keep stopping your workflow and go searching for a pen or other items that you need, focusing on the task at hand is much easier to do. Once you develop that focused momentum, your productivity is going to flow naturally.

- **Keep Track of Your Tasks** - Start tracking how long you spend on each task. This will optimize the time that you spend on a task and eliminates the mistake of spending far too much time on one task alone. It makes it easier to evaluate your work when you do this because you won't be falling into the trap of spending far too much time on unnecessary tasks. An even better strategy would be to get yourself a physical clock you can prop right next to your desk. To become more productive, your clock on your phone is not going to do it. Oh no, you need to go the old-fashioned route and go with a traditional physical clock. That's right, a clock that is propped on your desk right in front of you. This way, you're less likely to lose track of time. When you're continuously aware of just how much time you have left, it reminds you not to procrastinate. Once you've allocated a certain time-block to get things done and you have that physical clock in front of you to remind you, your brain automatically starts to focus on getting things done. This is by far one of the most effective ways to track your tasks properly and to be sure that you're spending just the right amount of time per task.

- **You Don't Need to Fear Technology** - Don't be afraid to embrace every app or piece of technology that is going to help with your productivity. The key phrase here is *"help."* Anything you choose to use should be to help you, not distract you. Rely on apps that help you keep track of your tasks and set up reminders and work-related notifications. If writing on a piece of paper doesn't work for you because it's easy to misplace, then put it on a to-do list on an app. All the resources you need to be more productive should be at the tip of your fingers and ready to do.

- **Schedule Breaks for Yourself** - Productivity does not mean that you need to work for eight hours straight before you can be considered productive. You're not a computer or a machine, you are a person with a limited supply of energy. Occasionally, that energy needs to be recharged to feel refreshed and ready to go again. As driven as you are to be as productive as possible, you also need to remember to take care of yourself. Handling one task after another in a row with no break time is a one-way destination to burning out quickly. Yes, you would quickly like to go through your task list and get everything done and over with as soon as possible it is still important to give yourself time to recharge between each task by taking the needed breaks. This is called buffer time, and when scheduling your tasks for the day, it is important that you leave some buffer time in between to allow yourself to recharge your mental energy. Getting a lot of sleep, rest, and exercise, is how you maintain a mind that is sharp, alert and functioning well, so well that it can handle any challenge that comes along.

- **Surround Yourself with The Right People** - Surrounding yourself with people who have the same mindset and ambitions that you do is going to make all the difference in the world. Working alongside them is going to skyrocket your productivity levels. You'll feel rejuvenated from the energy you get from them as you work together and bounce ideas back and forth. Make it your purpose to find people who inspire you to work and stay on track to achieving your goals.

- **Build the Habit of Saving No** - Sometimes, you need learn how to say no if it means putting yourself and your needs first. As much as you would like you, you cannot please or help everyone, and there will be some moments when you have to step up and say no. This is even more so when you have too much on your plate as it is. If you have to say no for some reason, you don't have to feel bad about it. It is impossible to please everyone else's needs and *still* finish your projects on time. The tasks that you have on hand right now should be given attention and priority until they have been completed, and unless they are not marked important, if you already have your hands full, then learn to say no. Get used to the idea of saying no to friends, family, or colleagues if their request is going to interfere with your working habits. You can help out when someone needs it, but only *after* you have finished your own tasks. If someone comes around asking for a favor that you simply don't have time for, then you need to politely decline or schedule it for another time.

- **Choose to Be Proactive Instead of Reactive** - Don't let the other distracting tasks dictate your day. There is always going to be another email and another notification that is going to come around. Instead of succumbing to these distractions, you could take the proactive approach by planning ahead and then sticking to that plan. It is always better to be well-prepared than to just wing it or go with the flow. You don't even have to go too far just planning ahead the night before even is sometimes enough. Take the proactive approach by getting involved in your own schedule instead of letting other factors decide it for you.

Ultimately, it is up to you to define and organize your priorities. Once you have your to-do list and determine how much time you have to work on the items of the list for today, then it is up to you to organize these tasks based on their priority. Important tasks should always come first because the important tasks are the ones that have consequences when you don't complete them. That is something to keep in mind as you now get to work on setting goals that you want to achieve.

Setting Goals to Achieve

Accomplishing goals is always going to seem hard when you have trouble staying focused and staying productive. But imagine how different it is going to be when you *can* stay focused and productive? You can accomplish more than you ever thought possible *if* you go about it the right way. If you have been notoriously bad in the past at setting and accomplishing goals, you're probably wondering how it is going to be any different this time around. Well, *it is* going to be different because the *approach* that you are going to take this time will be better than anything you've done in the past. After all, there is a good reason why you decided to pick up this book and get started. If you're wondering whether setting goals is an important part of the overall time management concept, the answer is *yes*. This is an important time management concept, especially when you are aiming to accomplish multiple goals and outcomes within a day. It is necessary to then determine what goals are the most important out of all the goals you have set for yourself for that day.

Setting your goals and objectives sounds like a step that is simple enough, and yet you would be surprised at how many people fail to do it properly. This will then give you the focus that you need to achieve these goals. Every goal that you set must be clear so that it will provide you with the focus that you need. Once you've established your goals, make a list of what is going to happen if you fail to meet your goals. This helps you stay on track towards accomplishing the tasks that you're supposed to, especially in a work environment where meeting deadlines is of the utmost importance. The best type of goal to set for the greatest level of productivity is the *SMART* goals system. Everything about the *SMART* Goals system just screams efficiency and productivity. Using *SMART* goals is a great way to get you motivated to start planning all the steps which you need to take to turn it from merely a goal, into a reality. You will always seem to fall short of your goals if it is not set the *SMART* way. Let's take a closer look at this acronym:

- **"S" Stands for Specific** - Smart begins by setting goals that are as specific as possible, down to the smallest detail. This is one of the most important parts to begin establishing the rest of your goals. When your goal is not specific, it is going to be increased to figure out if the goals you set are attainable or not. Specificity should be the main objective before you set out to create each goal. Every goal needs to be clear and well-defined. If you don't know what you want right from the start, you're not going to have much luck down the road trying to carry out your goals anyway. You can only get to where you want to be by defining precisely how you are going to get there.

- **"M" Stands for Measurable** - When you're thinking about how to measure your goal, the question you need to ask yourself is this: *"What will determine my success?"* Some goals can be measured with a simple yes or no answer, while other goals might require a little more detail to be deemed measurable. No matter what way you choose to measure your goal, it is important that the goal accurately reflects your success.

- **"A" Stand for Attainable** - An example of an attainable goal would be something like this: *"Within the next four months, I want to boost my productivity levels by fifty percent."* Attainable goals are realistic, and they will never feel impossible. When a goal is well-designed and specific enough, the action steps you need to take are going to be obvious. If the action steps are not clear, then you probably need to break down your goals into more manageable steps. Another common issue that prevents most people from accomplishing their goals are having too many goals at the same time. Don't fall into this trap and instead focus on working on one goal at a time if that makes you more productive.

- **"R" Stands for Relevant** - Your goals need to be relevant to what you want to accomplish. When you set goals, you need to ensure that they are relevant to your overall life plan too. If the goal you set is not going to benefit or better your life in any significant way, you might need to reevaluate if the goal is worth the time and effort you plan to invest in it.

- **"T" Stands for Time-Bound** - The final important component of your goal-setting process is to make sure you set a realistic deadline for each goal you want to accomplish. Yes, the deadlines are a necessary evil. A deadline creates a sense of urgency that, when combined with the rest of the *SMART* structure, makes you more likely to achieve that goal.

The *SMART* Goals framework is the foundation on which all your goals are going to be built. It's like a house, in a way. Without a firm foundation, a house will not stand for long. It'll serve its purpose for a while, but eventually, it starts to fall apart because the foundation is no longer strong enough to support it. A goal needs to be SMART because it helps you set each goal as clearly and definitively as possible. It provides you with a concrete way of measuring your success, showing you if you're progressing forward or not progressing at all.

Chapter 4:

One Thing at A Time

Sometimes, you've got the productivity and motivation. What is lacking is the *energy* to do all the things that you want to do in a day. You're sleeping enough at night, and yet, you can't seem to break the cycle of tiredness that is keeping you trapped. The common feeling of general tiredness is something that affects millions of people all over the world. With how busy life gets and the increasing demands to perform both at work and in personal life, is it any wonder that we feel tired all the time? Productivity and better time management are not going to mean much when you don't have the energy anyway to carry out all the wonderful strategies you've learned by now.

Energy and Recovery

Every day, you are committed to recharging your phone. You wouldn't go to bed at night without first making sure you've charged your phone for the day and avoid leaving the house with your battery running low. Remembering to recharge your phone is easy, but recharging yourself is a different story. Let's say you slept well the night before, and you're starting the next morning with your battery charged to a hundred percent. When the alarm rings, you roll over and check your phone before you even brush your teeth. You're not the only one guilty of this bad habit. You're scrolling through social media, browsing and replying to emails while you're still in bed, and by the time you're ready to hop out, ten percent of your battery has already been depleted. You get ready for work, commute, spend your day in meetings, interacting with your coworkers, managing phone calls, and trying to get your jobs done all at the same time. All the while, your battery is draining in the background as the day keeps running.

When the batteries on our phones run low, we're immediately notified about it. We get an alert on our phones telling us that the battery is running low, and we immediately start hunting for a charger to replenish that precious battery life. Unfortunately, in real life, we don't get an alert or a notification that tells us when *our batteries* are running low. The problem is that throughout the day, your body and brain are sending you signs and signals that your battery is about to run out. The problem is that we don't stop or hit pause long enough to tune in to the way that we're feeling.

Besides getting enough sleep at night, there are several other habits you can adopt to start making a difference in your energy levels.

- **Start Eating a Healthy and Balanced Diet** - This is the foundation of your energy levels and one of the most effective ways of keeping your energy levels up throughout the day. Not only do you need to eat healthily, but you also need to be eating at the right time too. Eating your meals on time is the key to sustaining your energy levels throughout the day. Don't skip out on breakfast either, because your body has gone through at least seven to eight hours or more since its last meal. You need to have at least three consistent meals a day, and when you're feeling peckish in between your designated eating hours, pick up some healthy fruit instead. Aim to eat food groups that are rich in iron. When your iron levels are running low in your body, it can leave you feeling drained, tired, and run down. This is especially important for teenagers and women. Women are at a higher risk of losing iron during their menstruation cycles. Red meat, green vegetables, and fortified food groups like cereal are a good source of iron.

- **Start Exercising Regularly** - The most difficult part of any workout is actually the first fifteen minutes leading up to that workout. You could come up with fifteen different reasons and excuses why you can't or won't exercise. But the benefit of exercise is that when you do this regularly, your brain produces serotonin. This sends a message to your body's nervous system where happiness and wellbeing reside. The real reason we feel great when we exercise is that exercising makes the brain function at its best. In today's technology-driven plasma screen world, it is easy to forget that we were born to move. For a lot of us, we work behind a desk Monday to Friday. That is almost eight to nine hours of sitting behind a desk. When we get home, we're sprawled out on our sofas as we call it a day, relaxing in front of the television of the iPad. Movement has become so minimal in the last century that we have forgotten this sedentary lifestyle is not good for us at all. We evolved as hunter-gatherers. Exercise makes you feel good, even after a long day at work when you feel like there is nothing left in the tank. If you pushed yourself to exercise for at least twenty to thirty minutes, you will immediately notice a boost in your energy reserves once the workout is complete.

- **Stay Hydrated** - Experts recommend that you have at least six to eight glasses of water every day. This is in addition to the fluids that you get from your food. Watch your alcohol intake since this can quickly cause you to become dehydrated. You need to watch your coffee intake too. Yes, coffee or any caffeinated drink, for that matter, will give that extra kick in your energy levels, but you're going to develop a tolerance to it over time. Eventually, you're going to need more and more cups of coffee to get you through the day, and this is not going to be good for your body. It's easy to understand why we've become addicted to our morning cup of coffee. Next to oil, caffeine is the second most traded substance in the world. Most of us can't imagine starting the day without our regular, steaming cup of caffeinated goodness. When we're awake, a chemical called adenosine accumulates slowly in the brain. Adenosine is the very thing that is responsible for binding the receptors in the human brain. This is how the brain begins slowing down its activity. As the day continues to progress, more adenosine begins to accumulate and feel progressively tired as the day drags on. The more adenosine you have in the brain, the more tired begin to feel. We need sleep to help the adenosine levels slowly decrease until it leads to the gradual process of wakefulness. Wakefulness happens only once your brain and body have had enough rest. Since caffeine has a similar structure to adenosine, it competes and binds with the waiting adenosine receptors. However, since caffeine is not adenosine, you don't feel the effects of sleepiness, and this explains why we feel alert and awake after those first few sips of warm liquid. However, the downside is because you don't feel the effects of the sleepiness created by adenosine, the calming properties that are supposed to be brought on by sleepiness are not there either. With long-term use, your brain tries to compensate for this by creating more adenosine receptors, and this, in turn, leads to more caffeine consumption. Too much caffeine in your system is going to make it difficult for your brain to shut down at night and get the required sleep that it needs.

- **Start Meditating Regularly** - Meditation is an incredible way to recharge your body's energy levels. Meditation does for your mind what exercise does for your body. Meditation gives you the physical, mental, and emotional downtime that your body desperately needs to stop it from reaching the point of feeling burned out and fatigued. Among the benefits you stand to gain from regular meditation sessions include a reduction in your stress levels, an improvement in your concentration, and a focus on your cognitive and creative thinking skills. With greater mental clarity, you're able to make better decisions and solve problems. Meditation gives you an increase in self-awareness, happiness, and self-acceptance because meditation helps you reconnect with your inner self. It will help you learn to appreciate life more as you become more aware of your surroundings through mindfulness. You learn how to block out distractions in your life. Regular meditation is going to improve your breathing and your heart rate, and it helps you feel more connected to yourself. It helps regulate your mood and anxiety disorders, helps you sleep better at night, and helps lower your blood pressure levels. Increases serotonin production that will help improve your mood. Your problems seem more manageable when you don't let your mind get the best of you. It helps you regain emotional steadiness, improves your mental resilience against adversity and pain, and it increases your optimism levels too. Meditation also has an impact on your entire nervous system. It reduces the body's production of cortisol, the stress-related chemical. This is a fantastic approach to recharging your energy levels, and it is easy enough to do whenever you need it.

- **Cut Back on The Sugar** - Adults and children today eat far too much sugar. Yes, sugar is going to give you that initial buzz of energy, but you're eventually going to experience a "sugar low" when your sugar levels come crashing down. When that happens, you're going to feel tired, and you're going to feel drained. Cutting out sugar feels like a task that is easier said than done, and you're probably right. Since sugar is available in almost everything we consume, it can be hard to cut back on it. Instead, what you can do is to aim for healthy sugars or sugars that are found naturally in certain food groups like fruits. Try to cut back on the artificial and processed stuff instead.

- **Taking Too Many Supplements** - Relying on supplements is another unhealthy habit that is not very helpful for your energy levels. There are no supplements that can compensate for an unhealthy diet or lack of energy levels. Truth be told, most people don't need to rely on supplements to get a boost in their energy levels. You could easily increase your energy levels by maintaining a consistent and healthy diet.

It is time to be committed to recharging your body and mind the same way you are committed to recharging your phone every day. Otherwise, none of the productivity and time management tips in this book are going to matter.

How to Stay Focused and Manage Distractions

Staying focused and managing your distractions is going to require something from you: *You need to ignore your Sirens.* The call of the *Sirens* is taken from Homer's book *The Odyssey*. Most people are familiar with the story of *The Odyssey*. In the book, Ulysses, the protagonist of the story, was trying to get home. To make it home, he needs to maneuver through a stretch of water where sailors often meet their untimely death. Sailors who pass through on their ships are lured by creatures known as the *Sirens,* and their irresistible allure is the reason why the poor sailors often meet their doom by crashing against the rocks. Ulysses could have given up and accepted his fate, but he decided not to. Instead, Ulysses instructed his crew members to tie him up to the mast of the ship and then instructed everyone to cover their ears. It didn't matter how much he would yell at his crew to steer the ship toward the song of the beautiful *Sirens,* and Ulysses was adamant that the ship continue to stay on course and head home. In this context, your *"Siren"* would be your distractions. Procrastination happens when you're lured by the call of your "distraction items," and you sail toward those temptations. Before you sit down to do any task, make sure that your chosen environment is a *Siren-*free zone. Delete the social media apps on your phone if it has to come to that.

Need a hand managing your distractions to stay focused? Take a look at some of these strategies below:

- **Manage Your Attention First** - Before you manage your time, you need to manage your attention. The biggest attention-grabber you have is something that doesn't leave your side, even when you go to bed at night. It's your mobile phone. Unfortunately, part of managing your distractions is going to require a little bit of separation. You can't have your phone at your desk anymore because you're always going to be tempted to look or check it, even when your phone is on silent. Manage your attention by putting your phone away, somewhere out of reach. Put it in your bag, or leave it in another room on silent mode while you're working from home.

- **Focus on Effectiveness Instead of Efficiency** - It's easier to become unfocused and succumb to distractions when you're focusing on the *wrong thing. Effectiveness* means that you are doing all the right tasks, and you're doing everything that you *should* be doing to bring you one step closer to your goals. *Efficiency,* on the other hand, simply means that you're doing something really fast. You could be *efficient* and be busy at work, but that doesn't mean you are working on the *right things*. When you're not working on the right tasks, you're not effective.

- **The Four Quadrant System** - The four-quadrant system was created by Dwight D. Eisenhower. He was the 34th president of the United States, a five-star general, and the founder of NASA. The four-quadrant system is also called the *Eisenhower Matrix,* and it is still a system that is widely used today because of how effective it is. Everything on Eisenhower's to-do list would fall into one of four categories. Those categories are **Urgent and Important, Non-urgent and Important, Urgent and Unimportant, and Non-urgent and Unimportant**. Things that were **Urgent and Important** had to be dealt with first. These were things of high importance and value to Eisenhower that needed to be taken care of in a timely matter or that had a pressing deadline. In the second quadrant, Eisenhower would list things that were *important but not urgent*. This is the category that needs the most planning and attention. In the third quadrant are items that are *urgent but not important*. This category must be trimmed wherever possible. The last quadrant are items that are **non-urgent and unimportant**. These tasks simply do not need to be done and can be eliminated or pushed to the very bottom of the to-do list. To avoid procrastination, aim to spend more time in quadrant two since these would usually be items that are not extremely urgent, but they are in your big picture goals or vision, and this means they are important for your success.

- **Map Out How Your Day Is Going to Go** - We always work better when we have some sense of direction. One incredibly effective strategy is to have a planner on your desk that is open at all times. The best type of planner would be the one with categories already listed that make it easier to map out your day. Since you're going to spend most of your time working at your desk, having this visual map next to you is going to help you stay focused and combat any distractions that might happen along the way. If it is not in your schedule, then it can wait. If you have to leave during the day, take a snapshot of your planner and bring this visual map reminder with you on your phone everywhere you go. Some people work much better and stay focused when everything is broken down for them, and they have a specific direction they know they should follow until the end of the workday.

Don't Procrastinate

Avoid falling into the trap of thinking that you always have time and use that as a reason to procrastinate because we never know what might happen along the way. The only way to start making the most of your time for the sake of your time management skills is to choose to spend it differently. Prior to this, you might have wasted a lot of it doing menial things that were not going to benefit you long-term, or even if you barely got anything done at all because you procrastinated and found excuses not to get to it thanks to a lack of self-discipline, you need to do a complete turnaround and start spending it very differently. You don't want to wake up one day and suddenly realized that life has passed you by. You don't want to wake up one morning and wish there was more you could have done with your life. In other words, you don't want to wake up one day filled with regret.

To avoid procrastination, you need to focus on the fact that your time is valuable. Wasting time on tasks that are not going to add any value or bring you one step closer towards achieving your goals is where most people tend to stumble and fall. From this moment on, every task that you undertake should be aligned with your goals. It should add benefit to your life if you're going to be investing time and energy into it. Everything must add value to avoid wasting your efforts on something that is not going to do anything for you. When you see and understand the value in everything that you do, procrastination will no longer be a strong and tempting factor in the equation.

Getting rid of the urge to procrastinate starts with the mindful decision to nip the habit in the bud. Every time that you are tempted to put something off, you should stop, and think for a minute and ask yourself if this is the right way you should be spending your time. This is yet another reminder of why priorities are crucial to your success with better time management. Your priorities will give you better clarity about what needs to be addressed first, which ideally should be the tasks that are going to be the most beneficial to you. Without the active and conscious decision to stop procrastinating, it can become very easy to fall by the wayside and continually find reasons why you cannot get things done. Always ask yourself if you are spending your time in the best possible way for your benefit before you decide on a course of action. There's an old saying that goes, why put off tomorrow what you can get done today, and it couldn't be more apt in this situation.

When you procrastinate, you're lying to yourself. You *don't* have a lot of time the way you think you do. Time has a funny habit of quickly slipping through your fingers as soon as you put your guard down. Put a stop to the tendency to procrastinate once and for all with the following measures:

- **Reward Yourself for Parts of Your Project** - As committed as you might be to your goals, there is no denying we could all use a little incentive along the way to keep going, especially during the tricky bits. Once you have divided your project into smaller, bite-sized, manageable segments, reward yourself every time you overcome one block. Once you're feeling happy by the little boost that the reward gave you, start work on the next block and look forward to the next reward. Keep going using this approach, and before you know it, you would have reached the end of your task with plenty of time to spare because you *didn't* procrastinate. Just like the farmer who lured the donkey to keep moving forward by dangling a carrot at the end of a stick, you need to use that same approach to eliminate procrastination. Besides, you do deserve a little pat on the back for finishing any goal that you accomplish, even if it is a small one.

- **Start Your Projects with the Tasks You Like the Best** - The hardest part about starting any kind of project is, well, getting started. No one ever looks forward to doing something they don't like, and this also happens to be one of the major culprits behind the desire to procrastinate. That is why starting with something that you like is going to make this obstacle a lot less challenging. When you start with something you like, your brain is triggered to release dopamine, the hormone that makes you feel happy. Look at your task list and ask yourself: *What is the smallest, easiest, and most enjoyable task on this list that I can do?* Doing this is going to help you build that flow and momentum that will get you through the to-do list of the day without succumbing to procrastination. Start with the task that you are going to enjoy the most, and work your way up from there.

- **Set A Timed Deadline for Yourself** - In the event there is nothing on your to-do list that you particularly enjoy, the next best thing is to pick the easiest priority task on your list and then set a timed deadline for yourself. When you know you only have a set amount of time to work on something, the task immediately seems more bearable in your mind. This way, even if you were dreading it, you know that the task is going to come to an end in ten or fifteen minutes (depending on the deadline you set). For example, if you have a report that you know you need to work on but you're struggling to get started, tell yourself that you're only going to work on this project for an hour, and then you're done. Look at the time when you start, do your best, and by the time the hour is up, you know you can call it a day on the project. What is interesting about this strategy is that once you get started, most of the time you will want to finish it. You'll be spurred by the motivation to get it over with about halfway through the task most of the time, and even if you don't, at least you know you started something. That is definitely better than not starting at all. Take a break only when your time is up. Get up, stretch, walk around, check your phone, do anything you want that helps you feel relaxed. Take a breather, reset yourself, and then sit down again and get back to work. During the time block, though, you should block out any and all distractions no matter work. This is the only way you're going to overcome procrastination.

- **Harness the Power of "No"** – People are afraid of saying "no" because of the negative connotations that have become associated with the word. However, there is an exception to this rule. That exception happens when you need to put your priorities first. In other words, you have to learn how to say "no" to avoid getting distracted by *other people's* requests. Although you would like to help, if you have a deadline you are already committed to, saying "yes" would only be a distraction. A distraction that you cannot afford if you're trying to boost your levels of productivity. You need to set boundaries. There is a time and a place where you can say yes and when you have to say no. If the request for help or the small favor is going to deflect you away from your priorities, then this is one of the few times in life where you need to be comfortable with the idea of saying no. When you say no, you need to be firm about it. Don't waver and don't hesitate. Remind yourself that you have a priority you have committed to and stick to your guns.

- **Use Music to Help You Get in the Zone** - Spotify has been a lifesaver on many occasions, and it can be beneficial in overcoming procrastination too, as it turns out. You can find music for all sorts of occasions, and there is even a playlist already prepared on Spotify called *Deep Focus*. An even better idea is to invest in noise-canceling headphones for those times when you can't completely block out noise distractions. If you're in a noisy environment, you're not going to be able to listen to your music. Noise-canceling headphones are probably the best invention when it comes to trying to stay focused and concentrate. If calm, relaxing, soothing music helps you focus better, you get to listen to those tunes through your headphones instead of the chatter and the buzz that's going on around you. If you're going to have to listen to noise anyway, it might as well be a noise that helps you concentrate and not distract you.

Conclusion

Thank you for making it through to the end of *Time Management and Productivity*, let's hope it was informative and able to provide you with all of the tools you need to achieve your goals whatever they may be.

Accomplishing a lot in a short amount of time seems impossible, but if there is one thing successful people have shown us is that *anything* is possible with the right tools and strategies. They are nothing if not living proof that if you manage your time wisely and boost your productivity levels to the fullest, it is going to make all the difference in the world. If you want to accomplish more within a shorter period of time, and feel like each task you accomplished was productive and meaningful, time management is the only way to do it. Habits need to change, goals need to be set, and priorities need to be determined. That is the only way you are going to see any lasting kind of change.

Time management is one of your greatest abilities. All that is left to do is for you to unlock its tremendous potential. You know you have it within you now, and you know just what needs to be done, it is all up to you now to make the changes you need to harness the power of effective time management and watch as it transform your life. Remember, it is not about *how much* you do in a day, it is about *how well* you organize your time. You could have 10 items on your to-do list and accomplish all ten with time to spare at the end of the day if you follow every strategy that has been laid out for you in this book.

As always, there is no better time than *right now* to start initiating the kind of change that you hope to see. Don't procrastinate taking control over the power of your time any longer. It is what you *choose to do today* that is going to make the difference tomorrow. Make your to-do list, eliminate distractions, find a happy balance, and live the most productive life you could have ever dreamed possible.

Finally, if you found this book useful in any way, a review on Amazon is always appreciated!

Description

How well do you spend your time each day?

Why do we need to manage time? Some people say we need to learn how to manage time because we know that time is precious, and it should be used to its fullest potential if we hope to reap the benefits of time. Others might say that time is money, and that is why we need to manage it as best we can. Logically, if we did that, we should be maximizing on our earning potential.

Every day is the day that you have the power to be powerful, successful, driven, and motivated. Every day is the day that you have the power to achieve a goal that you have always dreamed of. Every day is the day that you have the power to be more productive. There are no limits in life except the limits that you place on yourself. If we *know* we need to better manage our time, *why aren't the habits we try to implement sticking?* Why do we keep falling back into old habits and time continues to slip away from us?

All the work that you do in a day requires time. The very act of pausing for a moment to think about how you are going to use your time is already going to improve your time management and increase your productivity levels almost immediately. One of the biggest reasons why tasks seem to slip through the cracks is because we are *not* using the right strategies to help ourselves become the master of our time.

Sometimes, you've got the productivity and motivation. What is lacking is the *energy* to do all the things that you want to do in a day. You're sleeping enough at night, and yet, you can't seem to break the cycle of tiredness that is keeping you trapped.

That is why *Time Management and Productivity* was created. It was for that very reason this comprehensive guidebook was written to help you track, manage, and eliminate the mistakes you have been making all this while that were compromising your productivity. The solution lies in learning how to better manage your time with the right time management strategies. Here is what you can expect from this book:

- Understanding the value of time
- Why time management is a workout you never knew
- Time management and leadership
- The important rules of time
- Common difficulties most people face and why they struggle with time management
- Strategies to be more productive
- Defining and organizing your priorities
- How to set goals to achieve
- How to stay focused and manage distractions
- Don't procrastinate

A small tweak like effectively planning for your day is a small tweak that can bring about big changes in your productivity and the way that you feel at the end of the day, as well as how much you manage to accomplish at the end of it. Avoid falling into the trap of thinking that you always have time and use that as a reason to procrastinate, because we never know what might happen along the way. Time management is one of your greatest abilities. The question is, are you ready to unleash its power?

Printed in Great Britain
by Amazon